STEM Projects in **MINECRAFT**®

The Unofficial Guide to
Using Tools in
MINECRAFT®

SAM KEPPELER

PowerKiDS press.

New York

Published in 2020 by The Rosen Publishing Group, Inc.
29 East 21st Street, New York, NY 10010

First Edition

Editor: Greg Roza
Book Design: Rachel Rising
Illustrator: Matías Lapegüe

Photo Credits: Cover, pp. 1, 3, 4, 6, 8, 10, 12, 14, 16, 18, 20, 22, 23, 24 (background) Evgeniy Dzyuba/Shutterstock.com; p. 4 Nigel Jarvis/Shutterstock.com; p. 5 Wolfgang Kaehler/LightRocket/Getty Images; pp. 6, 12, 14, 16, 18 (inset) Levent Konuk/Shutterstock.com; p. 15 withGod/Shutterstock.com; p. 18 Morrowind/Shutterstock.com; p. 22 Ant Clausen/Shutterstock.com.

Cataloging-in-Publication Data

Names: Keppeler, Sam.
Title: The unofficial guide to using tools in Minecraft ® / Sam Keppeler.
Description: New York : PowerKids Press, 2020. | Series: STEM projects in Minecraft | Includes glossary and index.
Identifiers: ISBN 9781725310704 (pbk.) | ISBN 9781725310728 (library bound) | ISBN 9781725310711 (6 pack)
Subjects: LCSH: Tools–Juvenile literature. | Minecraft (Game) – Juvenile literature.
Classification: LCC TJ1195.K46 2020 | DDC 621.9–dc23

Manufactured in the United States of America

CPSIA Compliance Information: Batch #CWPK20. For Further Information contact Rosen Publishing, New York, New York at 1-800-237-9932.

Contents

Tools Through Time

People use tools every day. They use simple tools such as hammers and screwdrivers. They use not-so-simple tools powered by electricity and controlled by computers. Humans have used tools for as long as humans have existed! In fact, even humanlike creatures from earlier in history used tools. The oldest tools found are about 3.3 million years old.

You can use tools in the game of *Minecraft*, too. Some of the tools in the game have a lot in common with humankind's early tools. Early humans and humanlike creatures used **anvils** and cutting tools like axes. They were often made of stone.

Scientists found these stone tools, probably used for chopping things, in Tanzania. They may be more than 1 million years old.

First Tools

When you're playing *Minecraft* in Survival **mode**, what's the first tool you make? It's probably an axe or a pickaxe. You probably just use wood (sticks and wood **planks**) for that first tool, because wood is one of the easiest **resources** to find and collect. All you have to do is punch a tree! Once you have a wooden pickaxe, you can use it to get cobblestone to make better tools that last longer.

Axes work best on breaking wood blocks and things made out of wood. Pickaxes work best on all kinds of stone. Sometimes they work on metals, too.

MINECRAFT MANIA

To make most *Minecraft* tools, you'll need a crafting table. This block, crafted out of four wooden planks, might be the most important and useful block in *Minecraft*.

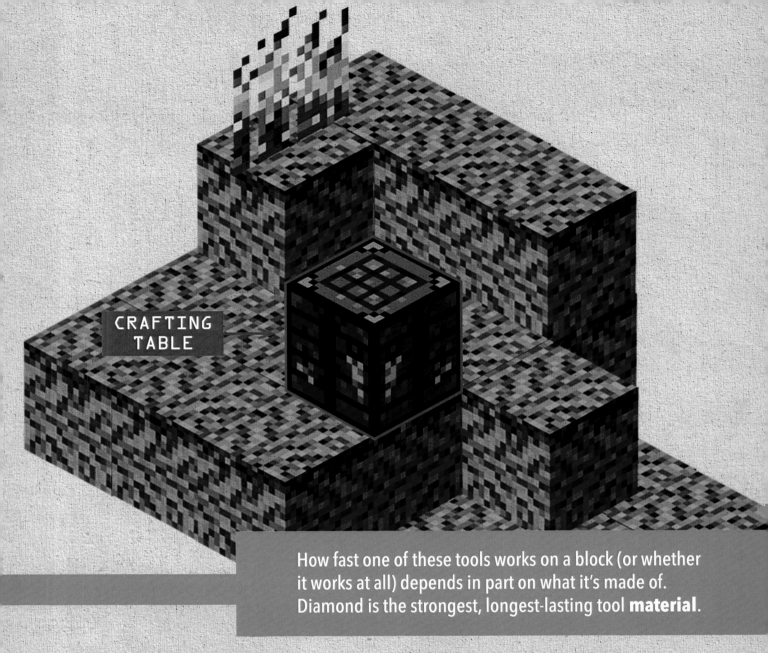

CRAFTING TABLE

How fast one of these tools works on a block (or whether it works at all) depends in part on what it's made of. Diamond is the strongest, longest-lasting tool **material**.

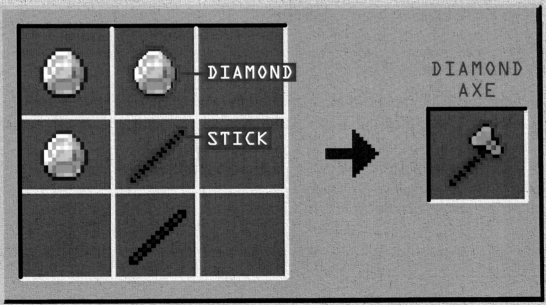

DIAMOND

STICK

DIAMOND AXE

Dig It

Another common early tool is the shovel. You can use shovels to dig through dirt, gravel, clay, and snow. You can also break these blocks using other tools or even your hands, but shovels are much faster. You can also tap grass blocks with a shovel to create a path.

The other first tool you'll probably make in *Minecraft* is actually a weapon. If you're playing Survival mode on any level other than "peaceful," you'll need a sword to protect yourself! Swords can be used as a tool as well. You can use them to break cobwebs into string.

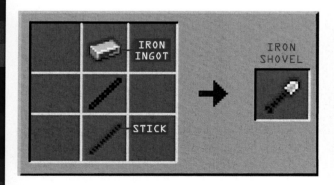
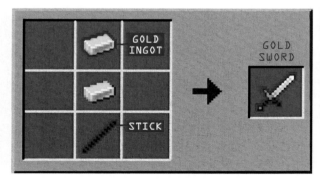

MINECRAFT MANIA

You can make tools and weapons out of gold **ingots** in *Minecraft* too. In fact, sometimes gold tools work faster than diamond ones! However, gold tools don't last long at all—not even as long as wooden tools do.

Snow blocks in *Minecraft* drop snowballs if you break them with a shovel. With four snowballs, you can craft a new snow block.

Shear Usefulness

Humans first **domesticated** sheep about 7,000 years ago. Today, there are about 1 billion sheep in the world! We raise these farmyard creatures for their meat and their wool. Their fleece, or coat of wool, is removed by cutting it off with tools called shears.

There are shears and sheep in *Minecraft*, too. You can make shears with two iron ingots. If you use shears on a sheep, it will drop one to three blocks of wool. You can use this wool for many things, including making banners, carpets, paintings, and beds that let you sleep through the night.

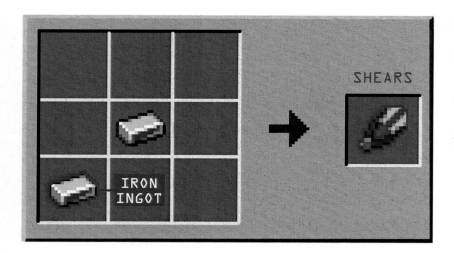

MINECRAFT MANIA

You can also use shears to gather cobwebs, vines, leaves, grass, seagrass, and ferns. You can use them on a pumpkin to turn it into a carved pumpkin and get pumpkin seeds.

Most *Minecraft* sheep are naturally white. A few spawn with gray, black, or brown wool.

11

Catching Fire

Fire is very dangerous both in the real world and in *Minecraft*! However, it can be very useful too. Early humans learned how to make fire about 9,000 years ago. They first used it to cook food and to keep warm. Early fire-starting methods included hitting a piece of flint—a hard, dark rock—against another material to create a spark. Today, people still start fires with flint and steel.

Flint and steel can start fires in *Minecraft,* too. You need a piece of flint and one iron ingot to make this tool. Be careful, though—if you're playing in Survival mode, you could burn yourself!

MINECRAFT MANIA

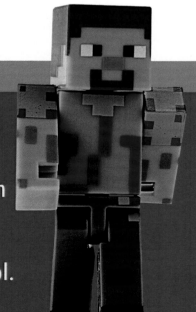

Many blocks in *Minecraft* will catch on fire, but the fire will go out quickly unless it's on a flammable block. This means a block on which fire can spread. These blocks include things made of wood, coal, leaves, and wool.

A forest fire in *Minecraft* can spread fast! Be very careful with flint and steel in the game—and never play with fire in real life.

A Row to Hoe

One of the oldest tools used in human agriculture, or farming, is the hoe. This tool has a blade sticking out from a long handle. The blade today is usually made of metal, but older hoes had wooden or stone blades. They're used to work with soil and remove weeds.

To do any farming in *Minecraft*, you'll also need a hoe. It can have a blade made of wood, stone, iron, gold, or diamond. Use a hoe to till dirt into farmland. Then you can plant crops, such as wheat, potatoes, carrots, melons, and pumpkins, in it.

MINECRAFT MANIA

You can also use a *Minecraft* hoe to turn coarse dirt into regular dirt. Coarse dirt is found in a few **biomes** and won't grow grass.

Hoes are still used in agriculture today. This person is hoeing a garden.

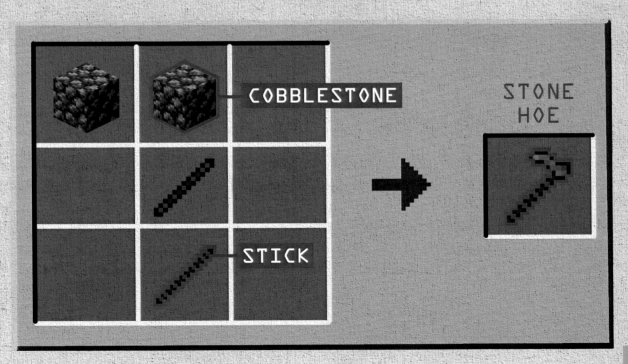

COBBLESTONE

STICK

STONE HOE

Fishing for Food

For thousands of years, humans have fished for both fun and for food. The ancient Egyptian and Chinese peoples fished with types of fishing poles, as did people from other civilizations. A fishing pole is also a tool in *Minecraft*. Not only can you catch fish for food with it, you might catch some other very useful resources.

You can fish in any size pool of still water in *Minecraft*. Throw your line in and wait. When you see a trail in the water, be ready! When the bobber goes under the water, pull in the line and see what you caught.

MINECRAFT MANIA

You can also catch fish in buckets in *Minecraft*. Just use the bucket on a fish swimming around in the water. Then you can carry it to a new body of water.

Cod is the most common fish to catch, followed by salmon. You might also catch treasure, such as **enchanted** books or items—or junk, such as rotten flesh, bowls, or bones.

Clock and Compass

In real life and in *Minecraft*, some tools are very simple. Some tools are a little more **complex**. Compasses and clocks are both tools that are old, but not as old as some of the simpler tools. Real-life magnetic compasses point north. People have used simple compasses since at least the 12th century. In *Minecraft*, compasses always point to your **spawn** point. Clocks that measure and show time have been around nearly as long as compasses. In *Minecraft,* clocks show you when the sun will rise and set. This is important when it comes to avoiding monsters!

<-- **compass**

MINECRAFT MANIA

European and Chinese sailors may have been the first to discover how to make simple compasses. Knowing your direction is important when you're out at sea.

You can create even more complex tools in *Minecraft* by using redstone and other items. Some people have even created working clock towers!

Repair Work

As you use them, *Minecraft* tools wear out just like real tools. However, you can repair them with other items and tools. Two worn-out tools of the same kind, such as stone pickaxes, can be combined with a crafting table. These tools won't keep any enchantments. You can also use an anvil—or a grindstone in some types of *Minecraft*. These tools will let you keep enchantments or combine them.

Humans have used real-life anvils and grindstones for many years. People used grindstones to sharpen stone tools and grind food items back in **prehistoric** times! By **medieval** times, people used round, spinning grindstones to sharpen knives.

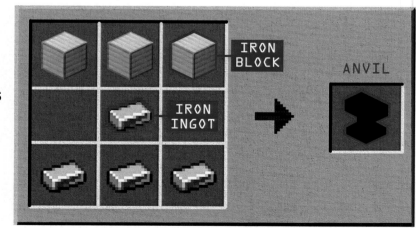

MINECRAFT MANIA

You can use an enchanted book with an anvil to add an enchantment to a tool. This takes experience points.

You can also find grindstones in some *Minecraft* villages. Weaponsmith villagers use them.

GRINDSTONE

Making Mods

You can make your *Minecraft* creations even more exciting with modifications, or mods. Using a computer program called ScriptCraft, you can create new blocks, change the way the game functions, and make your own games. Imagine what you could create! You could make pickaxes from emerald or lapis lazuli. You could create new and different tools to let you do even more building!

If you're interested in learning how to create mods in *Minecraft*, visit the website below. You'll find the information needed to get started with ScriptCraft and build your own *Minecraft* mods.

https://scriptcraftjs.org/

Glossary

anvil: A heavy iron block on which metal is shaped. In *Minecraft*, an item made from 31 pieces of iron and used to change and repair items.

biome: A natural community of plants and animals, such as a forest or desert.

complex: Having many parts.

domesticate: To breed and raise an animal for use by people.

enchanted: Having a magic spell placed on it.

ingot: Metal made into a shape for storage or transportation.

material: Something from which something else can be made.

medieval: Having to do with the Middle Ages, a time in European history from about 500 to 1500.

mode: A form of something that is different from other forms of the same thing.

plank: A heavy, thick board of wood.

prehistoric: Having to do with the time before written history

resource: Something that can be used.

spawn: To bring forth. In video games, when characters suddenly appear in a certain place.

Index

A
anvil, 4, 20
axe, 4, 6, 7

C
clocks, 18, 19
compasses, 18
crafting table, 6, 7, 20

D
diamond, 7, 8, 12

F
fishing pole, 16
flint and steel, 12, 13

G
gold, 8, 12
grindstone, 20, 21

H
hoe, 14, 14

I
iron, 8, 10, 12, 14

P
pickaxe, 6, 20, 22

R
redstone, 19

S
shears, 10
sheep, 10, 11
shovel, 8, 9
snow, 8, 9
stone, 4, 5, 6, 14, 15, 20
sword, 8

W
wood, 6, 8, 12, 14
wool, 10, 11, 12

Websites

Due to the changing nature of Internet links, PowerKids Press has developed an online list of websites related to the subject of this book. This site is updated regularly. Please use this link to access the list:
www.powerkidslinks.com/stemmc/tools